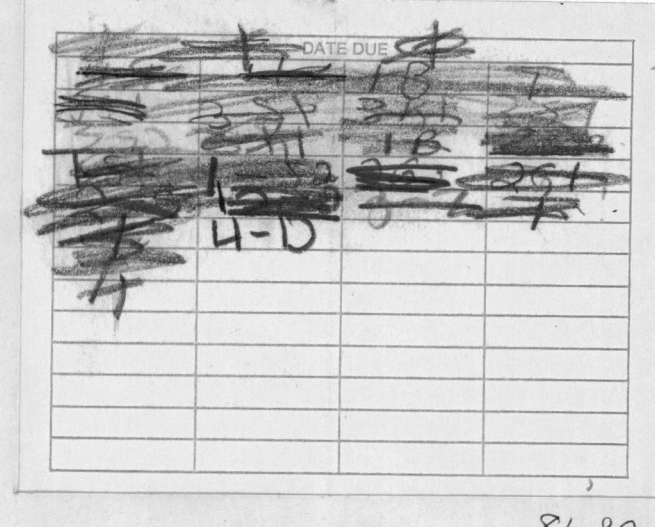

DATE DUE

GEMS AND MINERALS

GEMS AND MINERALS

BY SUSAN HARRIS

AN EASY-READ FACT BOOK

FRANKLIN WATTS
NEW YORK/LONDON/TORONTO/SYDNEY/1980

Thanks are due to the following for kind permission to reproduce photographs: J. Allen Cash; Anglo-American Gold Investment Company Limited; Asprey Limited (Bond Street); British Steel Corporation; Cement and Concrete Association; Controller of Her Majesty's Stationery Office (photographs are Crown copyright); Cutex Limited; De Beers Limited; Director of the Royal Pavilion, Art Galleries and Museums, Brighton; Glass Manufacturers Association; Institute of Geological Sciences; Johnson and Johnson Limited; Northwood Publications Limited (photograph first appeared in *The Magic of Amber*); Radio Times Hulton Picture Library; Royal Doulton Limited; Seaphot Limited; Sotheby Parke Bernet and Company; Standard Telephones and Cables Limited; Trustees of the British Museum; David Usill

Cover illustrations reproduced by kind permission of De Beers Limited *(left)*, and Aspreys Limited *(right)*

Frontispiece: A selection of rough diamonds

Line illustrations by Ken Scott

Library of Congress Cataloging in Publication Data

Harris, Susan.
    Gems and Minerals.

    (An Easy-read fact book).
    Includes index.
    SUMMARY: Describes in simple language the characteristics and uses of minerals and gems.
        1. Precious stones—Juvenile literature.
2. Mineralogy—Juvenile literature. [1. Mineralogy.
2. Gems]   I. Title.
QE392.H37   549   79-18661
ISBN 0-531-03241-8

R.L. 3.4 Spache Revised Formula

Above: rough diamond as it is
found in the mine, next to a
cut and polished stone.
Right: gold Victorian bracelet
decorated with pearls, diamonds,
turquoise, and rubies.

The **Earth's crust** (top layer) contains almost 3,000
different known substances called **minerals.** Some
minerals are unattractive and worth almost nothing.
Others are beautiful and also very valuable.

Among the most beautiful minerals are
gemstones. They form sparkling **crystals.** When cut
and polished they become **gems.** The finest gems are
made into **jewelry** and **ornaments.**

Many people think **rocks** and minerals are the same thing. But in fact, they are not. Minerals are the **components** (parts) from which rocks are made. Each mineral has the same **composition** (makeup) all the way through.

A rock may contain several different minerals. **Granite,** a common rock, is made up of three minerals: **feldspar, quartz,** and **mica.** However, all granite rocks do not contain equal amounts of these minerals.

Two specimens of granite

A piece of quartz and some semi-precious stones

Quartz is a common mineral. It is made up of **atoms** (tiny particles) of the elements **silicon** and **oxygen.** These atoms are always joined together the same way in quartz.

For every atom of silicon there are two atoms of oxygen. Every piece of quartz has exactly the same composition.

7

As noted earlier, most rocks may contain several minerals. But **chalk, limestone,** and **marble** contain only one mineral. This mineral is called **calcite.**

Calcite is composed of **calcium carbonate,** a white powdery **compound** (mixture).

Calcite crystals

Although there is only one label on this Iceland spar, it looks as if there are two.

One form of calcite is called **Iceland spar.** A piece of Iceland spar is very interesting. You can look through it. And when you look through it you see double (two images).

This is known as **double refraction.**

Minerals vary in **hardness** (resistance to scratching). Every mineral has a hardness that never changes.

Sometimes minerals look alike. They can be **identified** only by their hardness.

Mineral hardness is measured on a scale that runs from 1 to 10. It is called the **Mohs Hardness Scale.**

Talc, one of the softest minerals, is used to make talcum powder.

Mohs Hardness Scale

1. Talc
2. Gypsum
3. Calcite
4. Fluorite
5. Apatite
6. Feldspar
7. Quartz
8. Topaz
9. Corundum
10. Diamond

A **diamond** is the hardest of all. The only thing that can scratch a diamond is another diamond. A harder mineral can always scratch a softer one.

Minerals are easiest to recognize in the form of
crystals. There are six basic crystal shapes.
They vary from mineral to mineral. But each mineral
has a typical crystal shape.

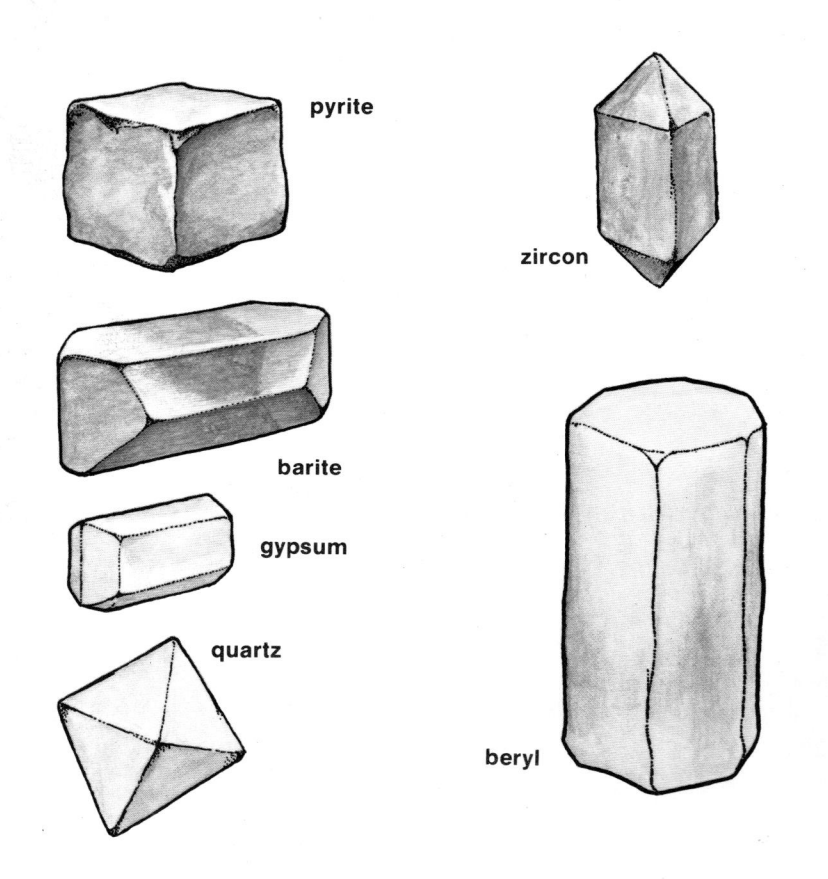

pyrite

zircon

barite

gypsum

quartz

beryl

The best crystals are found in **cavities** (empty spaces) in rocks.

Geodes lined with quartz crystals

Crystals are very nice when found in the cavities in small lumps of rock. These lumps are called **geodes.**
   Crystals appear in many different forms.

Twinned crystals

Sometimes a crystal seems to grow out of another.
This is often called a **twinned** crystal. Feldspar is a
mineral that forms twins.

   Mica crystals can split into thin sheets. Crystals that
do this are said to show **cleavage** (separation).

Mica crystals showing signs of cleavage

Mica is **heatproof** (not affected by heat) and **transparent** (see-through). Some is used as windows in boilers and heaters. This kind of mica is often called **isinglass.**

   Hematite, an **iron ore,** is found in several forms. It is often found in kidney-shaped masses. Then it is called **kidney iron ore.**

Kidney iron ore (hematite)

Not all crystals are transparent. Some minerals form crystals that look like metal. **Pyrite** is an example of this.

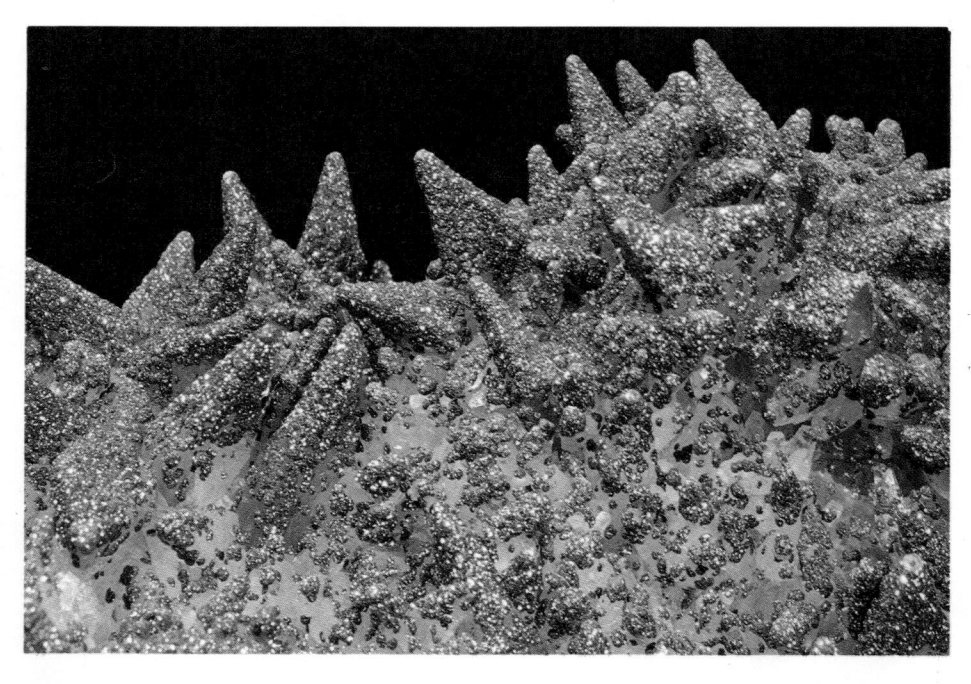

Pyrite crystals on a piece of calcite

Pyrite forms large yellow lumps that look like **gold.** Many people are fooled into thinking pyrite is gold. That is why it is often called **"fools gold."**

Sphalerite is an interesting mineral. It has also been called **blende,** and sometimes **black jack.**

Sphalerite

Sphalerite comes in brightly colored crystals, as well as black. It is an important mineral because it is an ore. An ore can be processed into metal. Sphalerite is an ore of zinc.

One of the most useful metals is iron. Iron is also the main part of many other metals, like steel. Iron is obtained by **smelting** (heating the ore in a furnace). The ore is usually heated with **coke** and **limestone.**

Smelting takes place in a **blast furnace.** A blast furnace is a large 200-foot (60 m) high structure. Its fiery temperature can go as high as 2,912 degrees F (1,600 C).

When iron comes from the blast furnace it is called **pig iron.** It is impure and must be **refined** (purified) in another furnace.

Molten (melted) iron leaving the blast furnace

A forging press shapes the red-hot steel

After refining, pure iron can be made into steel. Iron mixed with **carbon** and other metals becomes steel.

Steel is the main material used in building construction. Over 700 million tons of it are made every year.

Smelting is a common way of obtaining metals from their ores. **Copper, lead, zinc,** and **tin** are all obtained by smelting and refining in furnaces.

Some metals occur naturally in rocks, and are thus minerals.

These metals include gold, **silver,** and copper. They do not need to be smelted. But they may need to be purified.

Called **native elements,** they were the first metals used by humans. People have been using them for thousands of years. They make coins, jewelry and ornaments from them.

**Eagle made of gold,
with a crest
of diamonds**

Goldsmiths of the 1500s. The worker in front is beating the gold.

Silver and gold can be easily shaped. Shaping is done by bending and hammering.

Gold can be beaten into a sheet so thin it is almost transparent (see-through). Then it is called **gold leaf.**

Because gold is soft, other metals like silver are usually added to make it harder.

The purity of gold is stated in carats. The purest is 24 carats. Next comes 18 carats, or 75 percent gold. The most popular gold for jewelry is 14 carats.

Gold is considered rare. It is 58th in the order of abundance of elements (contents) in the Earth's crust.

Gold is sometimes found in the form of **nuggets** (lumps). The largest nugget was found in 1872. It weighed $472\frac{1}{2}$ pounds (214 kg). Most gold nuggets do not weigh even one ounce.

Gold is usually associated with wealth. Many countries keep part of their wealth in the form of gold. This is usually in **bars,** known as **gold ingots.**

Weighing gold ingots, or bars

Marks of the London Assay Office (place where object is registered).

Standard mark for sterling silver (shows quality of silver).

Date mark. This mark is for the year 1578–79.

This hallmark is the special mark of the maker or manufacturer of the object.

A variety of silver objects. The diagrams (right) show some typical hallmarks.

The most common form of silver is **sterling** silver. This is silver with 8 percent copper added.

Most gold and silver objects have a **hallmark.** A hallmark is an identifying mark. It shows when and where the object was made.

A hallmark is usually stamped on the back or on the bottom.

Copper is a much more common metal than silver or gold. Copper objects have been found among many ancient ruins. It was probably the first metal used in early times.

Some copper is found as a native metal. Most of it is obtained from its ores.

Copper **conducts** (passes) **electricity** very well. It makes good electrical **wire,** and fine **pipes** for household plumbing. Jewelry and ornaments are also made from copper.

Unfortunately, copper must be polished frequently to keep its bright color.

Far left: an underwater cable showing the copper wiring. Left: this bronze candlestick was made in the late 1200s.

A painting of the kitchen in the Royal Pavilion,
Brighton, England. Hanging in the background are copper
pots and pans, widely used in the early 1900s.

Copper is also a good conductor of **heat.** It has been
used for hundreds of years to make pots.

We see copper in our pennies.

We also see **alloys** that look like copper. An alloy is
a **mixture** of metals.

Bronze is copper containing some **tin.**

Brass is copper mixed with **zinc.**

Most other minerals contain metals, but they are not ores. This means they are not used for the metals they contain. However, these minerals can be made into important substances.

Halite is a mineral we use every day. It is **table salt.**

Salt is the chemical **sodium chloride.** It is found in sea water and as crystals in rocks.

Salt pans (basins) in Africa

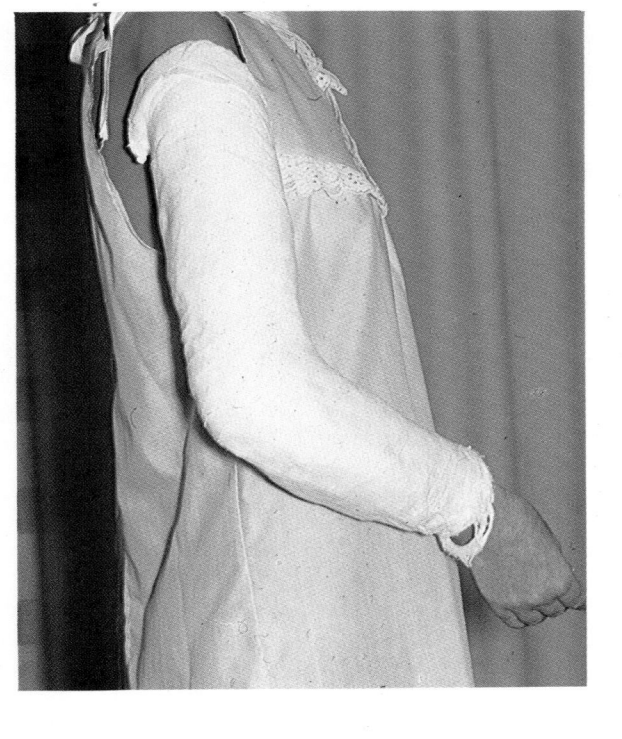

Woman with her arm in a plaster cast. The cast holds her injured arm stiffly, which helps the healing process.

Gypsum is the chemical **calcium sulphate.** It looks very much like **chalk.**

Gypsum is used for a number of things. It is an important ingredient in **cement.**

Mixing heated gypsum with water makes **plaster of Paris.**

When molded around a broken limb, plaster of Paris forms a stiff cast.

An important mineral is **calcite, or calcium carbonate.** It is the main chemical substance in **limestone.** It is one of the ingredients used to make **glass** and steel.

Calcite is also commonly seen in the form of **powdered lime.** Gardeners and farmers use this to improve their acid soils.

Another widely used mineral is **quartz.** It is a very common mineral. It is found in many rocks and mineral deposits.

Quartz is the main ingredient in glass. Quartz is also one of the main substances in **concrete.**

A glass-blower must shape the glass while it is in liquid form.

Pumping concrete on a building site

A widely used group of minerals are the **silicates.** They make up most of Earth's crust.

　　Clays are silicates. **Kaolin** is a pure clay mineral, also called **china clay.**

China figurines

It is called china clay because it is used to make dishes and figurines.

Another interesting silicate is **asbestos.** Asbestos is a special form of several silicates. It contains calcium, iron, and **magnesium.** It is in the form of long **fibers.** Asbestos is used to make fireproof materials.

Beryl crystals

Asbestos fibers

Some silicates form beautiful crystals. These are known as **semi-precious gemstones.** They include **garnet, topaz,** and **zircon,** among many others. When cut, they make lovely stones for jewelry.

Right: a selection of semi-precious gemstones

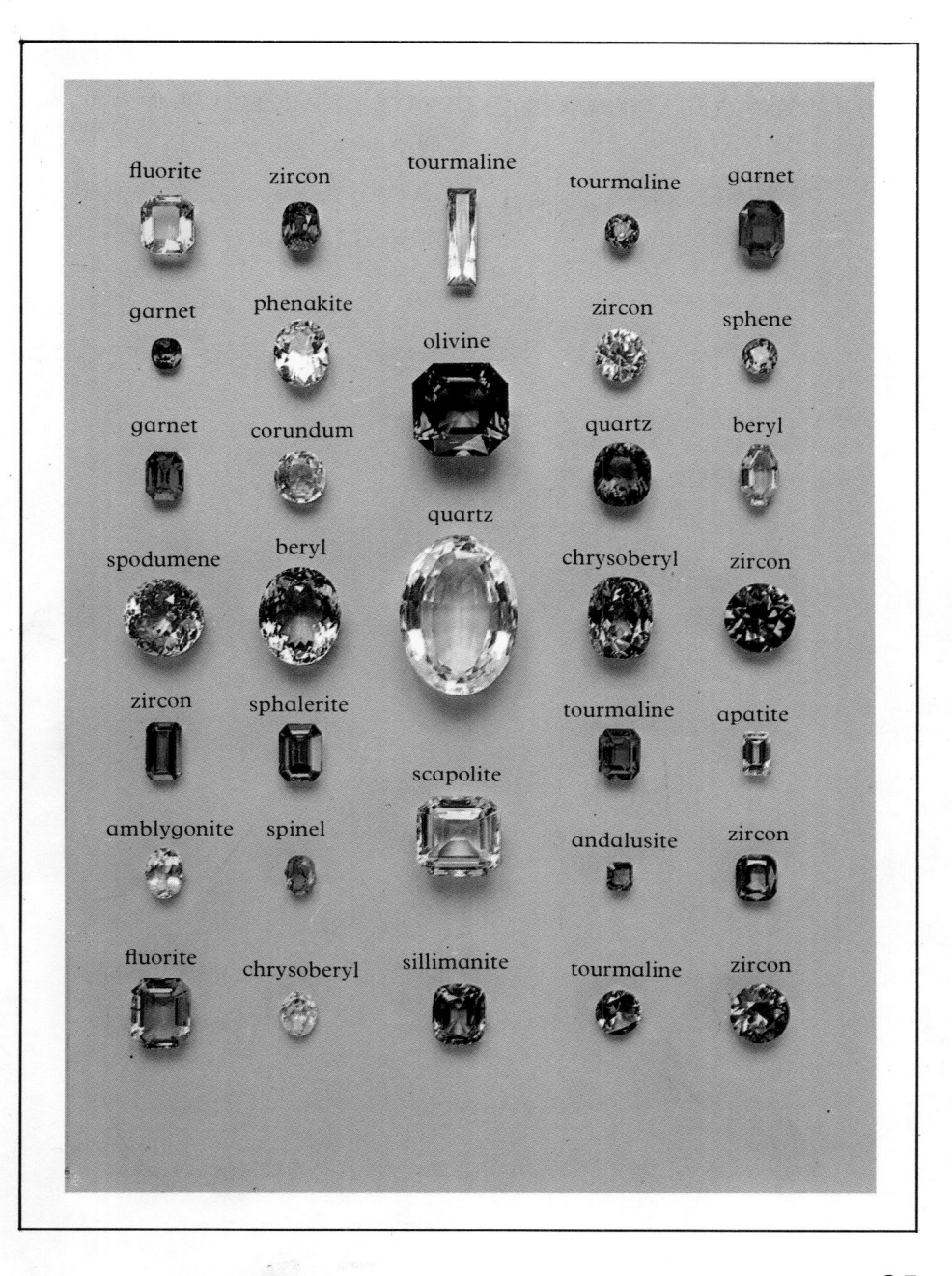

fluorite   zircon   tourmaline   tourmaline   garnet

garnet   phenakite   olivine   zircon   sphene

garnet   corundum   quartz   beryl

quartz

spodumene   beryl   chrysoberyl   zircon

zircon   sphalerite   tourmaline   apatite

scapolite

amblygonite   spinel   andalusite   zircon

fluorite   chrysoberyl   sillimanite   tourmaline   zircon

The most beautiful gems are diamonds. Diamonds are nearly pure **carbon** in **crystalline** form. When polished and cut, they flash and sparkle brilliantly.

Diamonds have a hardness that nothing else can match. And they are the most valuable **precious** stones.

Diamond necklace with a large emerald in the center

Diamonds come in many colors—pink, yellow, white, and blue. Blue diamonds are the rarest of all.

A geode cut in half by a diamond-bladed saw

Some diamonds are not good enough to be made into gems. These are called **industrial** diamonds. They are used in industry for cutting and drilling.

There are three other gems prized for their beauty and value. They are **emerald, sapphire,** and **ruby.**

The bright green emerald is a precious variety of the mineral **beryl.**

Sapphire and ruby are varieties of the hard mineral, **corundum.** Sapphire is a clear, deep blue; ruby a fiery red.

The pin (top right) is made of diamonds and emeralds; the bracelet (center) contains diamonds, emeralds, and sapphires; the earrings (bottom) are diamonds, with ruby centers.

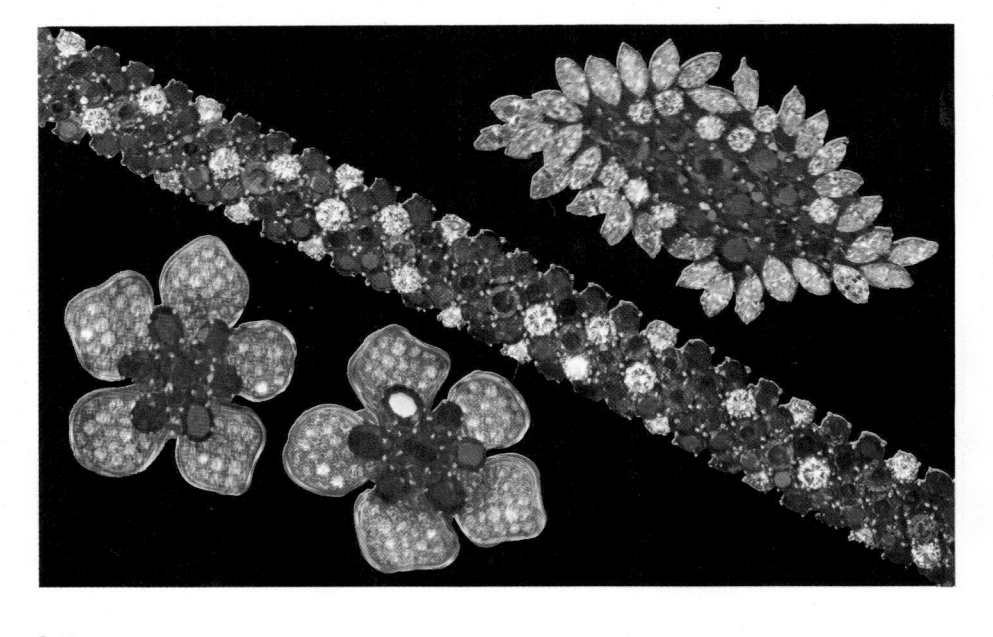

Top left: a diamond sorter wearing a special light in order
to see perfectly. Top right: cleaving (a method of
cutting) a diamond. Bottom: this machine is polishing a diamond.

Gem cutting has become a very special profession.
Over the years, gem cutters have studied the best way
to cut stones. It is an art to reveal a stone's true beauty
by cutting.

Diamonds are the most difficult to shape because
of their hardness. A diamond must be shaped by
grinding with **diamond paste** (made from other
diamonds).

Royalty have always looked for the finest gems for their crown jewels.

The British Crown Jewels are a famous collection. They are used at the coronations of British kings and queens.

The collection includes two huge famous diamonds. One is the **Koh-i-noor,** or "Mountain of Light."

The Koh-i-noor diamond is in the center of this crown, part of the British Crown Jewels.

The Star of Africa diamond, cut from the Cullinan, is shown in this scepter from the collection of the British Crown Jewels.

The other one is the **Star of Africa.** It is set in the sovereign's scepter, or staff. It was cut from the largest diamond ever found, the **Cullinan.**

The Cullinan diamond was found in South Africa, in 1905. It measured over $4\frac{1}{2}$ inches (11 cm) across. It weighed more than 21 ounces (600 g).

Not all gemstones are crystal-clear. Some are **opaque** (do not let the light through).

A selection of uncut opals, polished stones, and jewelry

They are beautiful because of their color and the way they reflect light.

Opal, similar to quartz, is one of the finest opaque gemstones. It has an unusual play of color known as **opalescence.** Opals may be green, turquoise, black, white, red, or orange.

Agate and **onyx** are varieties of very fine-grained quartz. Bands of color run through them. Playing-marbles are often made of agate.

Elephant made of lapis lazuli. The turquoise mask
(right) was worn by the Aztec Indians of Mexico.

An attractive semi-precious stone is the deep blue opaque **lapis lazuli.** It is a mixture of several minerals, but mostly **lazurite.**

    Turquoise, a greenish-blue stone, is very popular. It is so-named because it was originally found in Turkey. Turquoise is now found in various parts of the world.

A few gems are produced by living things.

The best known are **pearls.** Pearls form inside the shells of oysters.

Another is **mother-of-pearl.** It is obtained from the shell lining of **mussels, abalone,** and other **shellfish.** Mother-of-pearl is used to make buttons and other ornaments.

Pearl necklace, and a dish made of mother-of-pearl

A pearl starts to grow when a grain of sand gets inside the shell and irritates the oyster. For protection, the oyster covers the sand grain with layers of **nacre.** Nacre, a form of calcite, is also the shell lining. Very gradually a valuable pearl forms around the sand grain.

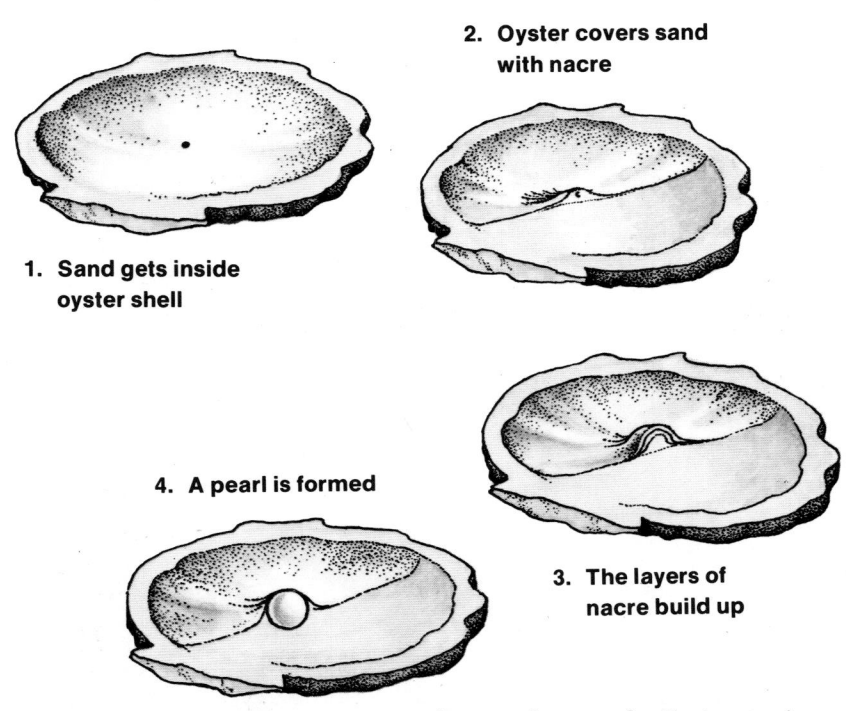

2. **Oyster covers sand with nacre**

1. **Sand gets inside oyster shell**

4. **A pearl is formed**

3. **The layers of nacre build up**

Another type of pearl is a **cultured pearl.** Cultured pearls are formed in the same way as precious pearls. But there is an important difference. People place grains of sand inside oysters in special **oyster farms.** This encourages pearls to form.

41

Coral is a tiny animal that lives in colonies in warm waters. It grows a chalky **skeleton** (framework). As these creatures die, others pile on top of them. The skeletons mount up.

Eventually the skeletons form **coral islands** and **reefs.** Coral comes in many colors. The red Mediterranean variety is the most valued.

Coral is quite soft. It can be carved to form attractive jewelry and ornaments.

Coral reefs

Coral statue

Jet vase

Amber, showing insects trapped inside

Amber, usually a deep orange, is a pretty gemstone. It is a **fossil resin.**

This resin is the sticky substance that oozes from trees. It has become hard **(fossilized)** because it is hundreds to millions of years old. Some pieces of amber have preserved insects trapped inside them.

Jet is also the remains of long-dead trees. It is a shiny black, clean form of coal. Jet is often shaped into beads.

Large amounts of minerals are used in the world every day. **Mining** (taking minerals from the ground) is a very important industry.

Sometimes mineral deposits are near the surface of the ground. Then the topsoil is removed and the deposit underneath shoveled up. This is called **strip mining.**

Open pit diamond mine in South Africa

Power shovel being used in the pit of an open mine

Many minerals are found in deposits thousands of feet below the earth's surface.

Huge machines are used to do part of the mining work. But people must still go down into the ground to work the machines.

Coal is a rock that is mined underground by people and machines. It is dark, dirty, unpleasant work, but coal is needed for many things.

45

Panning for gold in the 1900s

A very simple form of mining is called **panning.**

A miner puts gravel from a riverbed into a pan. Then the gravel is swirled around with water. The light gravel washes away. If there is any gold present, it is heavy and remains in the bottom of the pan.

Today, not many people use panning to look for gold in river gravels. Instead, dredging machines are used.

A great many minerals are found in veins, deep down in rocks. The minerals have to be extracted by **underground mining.**

In South Africa, some gold mines go down over 2 miles (3 km). The deposits have to be blasted from the rocks with explosives.

The next time you see beautiful jewelry, ornaments, or statues, stop and think. Remember all the human work that has gone into creating them.

Drilling for gold in a South African mine. Lower left: head of a golden buddha in Thailand. The buddha's large head and body contain 3 tons of solid gold.

INDEX